CONTEMPORARY LIVES

JUSTIN BIEBER

MUSICAL PHENOM

ABDO
Publishing Company

JUSTIN BIEBER

MUSICAL PHENOM

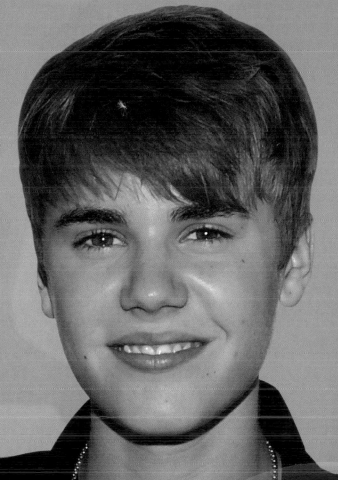

by Valerie Bodden

CREDITS

Published by ABDO Publishing Company, PO Box 398166,
Minneapolis, MN 55439. Copyright © 2012 by Abdo Consulting
Group, Inc. International copyrights reserved in all countries.
No part of this book may be reproduced in any form without
written permission from the publisher. The Essential Library™ is a
trademark and logo of ABDO Publishing Company.

Printed in the United States of America,
North Mankato, Minnesota
112011
012012

 THIS BOOK CONTAINS AT LEAST 10% RECYCLED MATERIALS.

Editor: Lisa Owings
Copy Editor: Chelsey Whitcomb
Series design: Emily Love
Cover production: Kelsey Oseid
Interior production: Marie Tupy

Library of Congress Cataloging-in-Publication Data
Bodden, Valerie.
  Justin Bieber : musical phenom / by Valerie Bodden.
     p. cm. -- (Contemporary lives)
  Includes bibliographical references and index.
  ISBN 978-1-61783-321-2
  1. Bieber, Justin, 1994---Juvenile literature. 2. Singers--Canada--
Biography--Juvenile literature. I. Title.
  ML3930.B54B64 2012
  782.42164092--dc23
  [B]
                          2011040467

TABLE OF CONTENTS

Justin Bieber performed at Madison Square Garden in August 2010.

CHAPTER 1
Crowd Pleaser

IIIIIIIIIIIIIIIIIIIIIIIIIIIIIIIIIIIIIIIIIIIIIIIIIIIIIIIIIIIIIIIIIIIIIIIIIIIIIIIIIIIIIIII

The excited shrieks of thousands of young girls filled the air of Madison Square Garden in New York City on the evening of August 31, 2010. The arena—which seats 20,000 people—was sold out. Everyone was there to see one person: teen singing sensation Justin Bieber.

Backstage, energy levels were also high as Justin and his crew prepared to put on the show of their lives. This would be the biggest concert of Justin's career. Headlining at Madison Square Garden is a major sign of success for a musician. In the past, the arena had hosted concerts by such legends as the Rolling Stones, U2, and Michael Jackson. At only 16, Justin had a lot to live up to with this performance.

Just before the show started, the Canadian artist linked arms with his mother and his crew to pray. Then Justin took his position under the stage and prepared to make his entrance. The crowd went even wilder as the purple-and-white clad Justin rose onto the stage inside a metal ball. The singer jumped into his first song, "Love Me," performing karate-like dance moves as he sang.

After performing his next song, "Bigger," Justin worked the crowd: "What's up, New York City? Welcome to my world. We are gonna have a lot of

INSPIRED BY

Although Justin has said he does not try to emulate other performers, a number of musicians have inspired him, including Michael Jackson, Stevie Wonder, Boyz II Men, Usher, Chris Brown, and Justin Timberlake. Other favorite singers include Ne-Yo, Taylor Swift, and fellow Canadian Drake. The singer also enjoys listening to hip-hop music by Lil Twist, Lil Wayne, Soulja Boy, and similar artists.

fun tonight. I got a lot of surprises in store for you guys!"[1] Then he brought out one of those surprises. The musical group Boyz II Men joined him for the song "U Smile" before singing their own hit, "On Bended Knee."

As the show continued, the crowd was treated to lasers, lights, and pyrotechnics. For the songs "Never Let You Go" and "Favorite Girl," Justin grabbed his acoustic guitar and took a seat in a heart-shaped metal cage that flew over the audience, triggering even more shrieks as the fans got a close-up look at their idol. As Justin climbed out of his heart, one lucky girl was brought onstage to join him. Justin presented her with a bouquet of flowers and serenaded her with the song "One Less Lonely Girl."

Then Justin brought out more musical surprises. Justin's mentor and friend, Usher, joined him for the song "Somebody to Love." Afterward, pop star Miley Cyrus stepped onstage to perform "Overboard" with Justin, followed by young star Jaden Smith, who came out for a rap during the song "Never Say Never." Later, singer Sean Kingston joined Justin for their hit "Eenie Meenie."

Between songs with other superstars, Justin sang several solos. He flew out over the crowd again during the song "Up" and played a baby grand piano for "Down to Earth." During scene changes, the crowd had a chance to ooh and aah over big-screen pictures of Justin's early life. At the end of his set, Justin headed backstage before returning for his encore, which included yet one more surprise—rap star Ludacris, who joined him on the fan favorite "Baby."

As fans held their hands in heart shapes above their heads and screamed his name, Justin left the arena. Backstage, he collapsed on a couch, exhausted from 75 minutes of almost nonstop singing and dancing. But as his friends and family came back to congratulate him, Justin was reenergized. The show had been a success!

PRESERVED IN WAX

In March 2011, Justin was immortalized—or at least his figure was. Wax statues of the star were put on display at Madame Tussauds wax museums in New York, Amsterdam, and London.

A team from the museums spent four months studying Justin's hair, eyes, and posture to get everything just right. Each figure was dressed in a different outfit donated by the star.

Justin's wax figures were designed to look as lifelike as possible.

THE CONCERT THAT ALMOST WASN'T

Only three days before his Madison Square Garden concert, it had looked to Justin's crew as though he might not be up to performing. His My World Tour had begun at the end of June, and already,

Even in the middle of his rise to stardom, Justin recognized everything was happening very fast. In his song "Up," he sang, "It's a big, big world. It's easy to get lost in it." He acknowledged that those lyrics might apply to his life. "My world got very big, very fast, and a lot of people expect me to get lost in it," he wrote in his memoir *Justin Bieber: First Step 2 Forever: My Story*.[2] But unlike other young stars who have turned to drugs, alcohol, or crime, Justin said he would not get lost because of the great support team behind him.

Justin had completed 38 concerts. The constant performances and nearly nonstop travel across North America had begun to take their toll.

By August 28, Justin's throat was sore—and his voice was showing it. Although he performed that night in Newark, New Jersey, a doctor insisted he be put on vocal rest afterward. That meant no singing and no talking. It also meant Justin would have to cancel a show scheduled for August 29 in Syracuse, New York. The teen star reluctantly obeyed the order to cancel the show, but he was upset at the thought of letting his fans down. To let his fans know he was thinking about them, he sent out a message through the social networking site Facebook:

> I know how much fans count on me, and I want them to know I care. . . . I don't want to let anyone down. Without my fans, I can't live my dream, and I will never take that for granted.[3]

After vocal rest, a strict diet (including no fast food), and hard work with his voice coach, Justin was ready to perform at Madison Square Garden.

TRUE BELIEBERS

From the beginning of his career, Justin was adored by millions of loyal preteen and teenage girls. Fans even came up with their own "Bieber" language. A *Belieber* is someone who believes in Bieber, *OMB* stands for "Oh my Bieber," and a *Bieberholic* is someone who is addicted to the star.[4] Justin acknowledged his fans' support, although he admitted to being puzzled by their obsession, saying he had no idea why fans screamed and cried when they saw him. Still, the star recognized that his fans had changed his life. As he said in a special thank you message on the video-sharing site YouTube in 2009,

"This is just the beginning, but I wanted you to know how thankful I am because without you this would never have happened."[5]

THE FAST TRACK

Some artists wait their entire careers to perform at a venue as renowned as Madison Square Garden. But Justin was first discovered by the recording industry only three years before his performance there. After his discovery, he struck a deal with a record label and released two hit albums, *My World* and *My World 2.0*. He traveled across North America and the world, performing in concerts, doing radio interviews, and taking part in television talk shows. He also racked up an enormous following on Facebook, MySpace, YouTube, and Twitter.

Sometimes when Justin reflected on how fast everything was happening, he was overwhelmed: "Every so often, I think, 'Wow.' But I don't know. I

MAKING THE GOAL

The summer before his concert at Madison Square Garden, Justin sat in the crowd at a Taylor Swift concert in the arena. Awed by the thousands of screaming fans there, Justin came to a decision—he would perform at the Garden in a year. Although his manager was not so sure that was possible, Justin insisted he would work as hard as was necessary to get there. And one year and three days later, there he was!

Justin was only 16 years old when he performed at Madison Square Garden with other stars, including Usher.

just don't think about it. I just take it one day at a time."[6] Lately, though, it seemed those days were becoming busier and busier. And sometimes, Justin felt like it was only the beginning.

||||||||||

Justin was raised by his mother,
Pattie Mallette.

CHAPTER 2

Young Musician

||||||||||||||||||||||||||||||||||||||||||||||||||||||||||||||||||||||||||

Justin Drew Bieber was born on March 1, 1994, in London, Ontario. He grew up in Stratford, a small town in Ontario, Canada. His mother, Pattie Mallette, was in her late teens when Justin was born. She split up with his father, Jeremy Bieber, when Justin was only ten months old. Soon afterward, Jeremy took a construction job in Winnipeg, and Justin saw him only once in a while.

As a young mother, Pattie often found it difficult to watch her friends go out while she stayed home to care for her new baby. She later reflected that she simply did what she had to do:

> I was young. I wanted to make sure that I gave him everything, that I would be the best that I could be for him. It was hard work, but it was worth it.[1]

According to Justin, his mom worked hard in order to make ends meet. At the same time, she provided discipline and a Christian upbringing that stressed the importance of having God in his life.

Although Justin and his mother lived in public housing and Pattie often struggled to keep food

LEARNING FROM MOM

Justin has always been close to his mother, who has been upfront with him about her past involvement with drugs, alcohol, and crime. She has also told him about how she began to believe in God after trying to commit suicide and how she gave up drugs and alcohol for good when she found out she was pregnant with him. Justin said knowing about his mother's struggles helped him appreciate and respect her even more. "I admire her so much for how she learned from her mistakes, got her life together, and made a life for me," he said.[2]

on the table, Justin later said he never felt poor as a kid:

> *I definitely didn't think of myself as not having a lot of money. . . . I couldn't afford to get a lot of new clothes a lot of times. But I had a roof over my head.*[3]

Pattie's parents, Bruce and Diane Gale, also played a big part in Justin's life. From the time he was a young boy, Justin was especially close to his grandfather, who taught him to look for the good in people and in each moment.

||||||||||||||||||||||||||||||||||||||||||||||||||||||||

GETTING IN HIS GROOVE

Whether Justin and his mom were in the car or at home, Pattie always had the radio tuned to her favorite music: rhythm and blues (R&B) classics by Michael Jackson, Stevie Wonder, and Boyz II Men. Many of Pattie's friends were musicians, and they often stopped by with their guitars to play and sing. By the time he was two years old, Justin began to show a flair for music himself. He drummed on pots and pans, the kitchen table, and even the couch. Pattie bought him a toy drum

Justin recognizes that it probably was not always easy for his mother to listen to his first attempts at music. But he is grateful she did, and he now calls on others to allow youngsters who want to play music to go for it—even if it doesn't sound beautiful at first.

He also encourages his fans to try things they are not sure they will be good at, without worrying what others will think. "If we do only the stuff we're good at, we never learn anything new," he wrote in his memoir.[4]

set and soon noticed he was keeping a beat with it. He was allowed to play the drums and other percussion instruments at church too.

When Justin was five years old, Pattie's friend Nathan McKay got a group of musicians together to perform at a local bar. They collected donations to buy Justin his first real drum set so he could play along with the radio at home. That summer, Justin joined the church band for a show at a local fair. He was so small the crowd couldn't see him behind the drum set, but they could hear him!

By this time, Justin had begun to play around on the piano too. Although he couldn't read music and didn't take lessons, Justin was able to play songs after hearing them on the radio or in church. He later tried to explain how:

> When I listened to music in church, I could feel those harmonies hanging in the air like humidity. It wasn't an issue of learning exactly: it was more as if the music soaked in through my skin. I don't know how else to explain it.[5]

Soon, Justin had begun to play guitar, and by the time he was nine years old, he was pretty good. His dad, also a guitar player, introduced him to rock songs such as "Knockin' on Heaven's Door" by Bob Dylan and "Give a Little Bit" by Supertramp. Later, Justin also began playing the trumpet, and when he was ten, he began singing around the house. Standing in front of the bathroom mirror,

HANGING WITH DAD

Justin's dad, Jeremy, lived more than 1,000 miles (1,610 km) away in Winnipeg, Canada. However, Justin and his father were still close. Jeremy visited Justin whenever he could, and the two sparred together (Jeremy was a former professional fighter) or played guitar. It was obvious Jeremy was proud of his son. He posted on his personal Web page, "My son is my life. He's nine years old, and he's the most talented person I know."[6]

he would belt Michael Jackson songs into a blow-dryer or Brian McKnight ballads into a toothbrush.

||||||||||||||||||||||||||||||||||||||||||||||||||||

A NORMAL KID

Justin attended elementary school at Jeanne Sauvé Catholic School in Stratford. The school was a French immersion school, meaning students didn't speak English at all during the school day. Every subject was taught in French so students would learn the language as they learned other subjects. Although such training made Justin fluent in French, it also made him self-conscious around his friends who went to public school. He was afraid they would think he was a geek. He wanted to be thought of as a regular kid, and his musical talent

LIVING HIS FAITH ||||||||||||||||||||||||||||||||||||||||||||||||||||||||||

Justin's mother raised him as a Christian, and he grew up going to church. Today, Justin prays with his crew before every performance and talks about God during his concerts. He said,

"I feel I have an obligation to plant little seeds with my fans. I'm not going to tell them, 'You need Jesus,' but I will say at the end of my show, 'God loves you.'"[7]

Justin also attests to being incredibly grateful to God for all of the blessings he has received.

In addition to music, Justin, *left*, also enjoyed hanging out with friends and playing sports.

was just one more thing that made him different. He decided to keep his music a secret, singing and playing only at home and in church.

Justin's friends knew him best for playing sports. He could often be found on the soccer field or at the hockey rink, usually with his best friends,

Chaz Somers and Ryan Butler, both of whom remain his pals today. When they weren't at school or playing sports, the three boys often spent time at Justin's grandparents' house, watching TV, kicking the couch cushions around, or wrestling. Justin could also be found skateboarding in Stratford's parks or wandering through Long & McQuade's music store. At school, Justin was a prankster and a class clown.

Even though Justin continued to hide his singing from his friends and didn't plan on doing anything with it, he knew he was good. He stated, "I was just a kid messing around and having fun. I wasn't taking any of it real seriously."[8] He and his mom would watch the hit show *American Idol* together, and he would always tell her he could

BULLYING JUSTIN

Justin was always small for his age, and that led some kids to try to bully him. But Justin's dad was a former professional fighter and had taught Justin how to defend himself. Although Justin preferred not to fight, he didn't let others push him around or say mean things about his friends. Justin would later sing about his early experiences with bullies in the song "Bigger": "Now the bullies in the schoolyard / Can't take our hugs and our kisses from us (No!) / Because we ain't pushovers no more, baby."[9]

INSTRUMENTAL PERFORMANCES ⁣||||||||||||||||||||||||||||||

Although Justin is perhaps best known for his singing and dancing, his early experiences with instruments continue to show up in his performances today. Nearly every show includes the star banging out at least one drum solo. He also plays acoustic guitar on several numbers and takes to the piano for the song "Down to Earth."

make it on the show. But at 12, he was at least four years away from being old enough to try out. His age wouldn't stop him from entering another singing contest though—one that would set in motion a stunning series of events.

||||||||||||

Some of Justin's biggest fans are from Stratford, Ontario, where Justin grew up and got his start in the music industry.

CHAPTER 3

Stratford Star

||||||||||||||||||||||||||||||||||||||||||||||||||||||||||||||||||||||||||||||||

J ustin has always loved being the center of attention. In 2007, he decided that entering a singing contest would give him an opportunity to do just that by singing for a crowd. He signed up for the Stratford Star, a local, four-week-long, elimination-style competition for children ages 12 to 18. Although most of the other singers in the competition were older than Justin and had years of voice training, Justin wasn't nervous. He said,

What's to be afraid of? The few people who knew me were people who loved me, and the rest were strangers, so if I didn't do well it wasn't like I'd ever have to see them again.[1]

For the first round of the competition, Justin sang the Matchbox 20 song, "3 a.m." When he finished, the audience cheered. It was the first time he'd had that experience—and he liked it. He made it past the first elimination and on to the second round. Next, he sang Alicia Key's "Fallin'," and for the third round, he performed Aretha Franklin's "Respect." His rendition of "So Sick" by Ne-Yo earned him a spot in the final three.

At last, it was time for the winner to be announced. Although Justin had originally entered the competition for fun, he now realized he really wanted to win. And then the emcee announced the winner's name. It was not him. Justin later wrote of that moment, "A little chunk of my heart fell out and rolled under the piano."[2]

Although he was disappointed by his loss, Justin still wanted to share his performance with family members who had not been able to attend the competition. He and his mother started a YouTube account and uploaded the videos Pattie had taken of Justin's performances. His family members loved the videos, of course—and so did complete strangers. Justin began receiving compliments from people around the world, along with requests for more videos. So Pattie got out the video camera and began filming Justin singing in his room or on the couch. Soon, Justin's videos had 100 views. Then they had 1,000. And the hit counter kept going up. Justin's popularity attracted the attention of Rapid Discovery Media, a Toronto-based company that helps performers maximize their Internet exposure. The company began to help Justin and Pattie produce and promote more professional-looking videos, boosting his number of YouTube views even higher.

DATING DISASTER

Although Justin is now the dream date of millions of girls around the world, his first date did not go so smoothly. He was 13 years old, and he took his date to a buffet restaurant, where he piled his plate with spaghetti. But Justin was nervous—more nervous than he would ever be on stage, he later reported—and he spilled the spaghetti all over his white shirt. Despite the disaster, Justin said afterward he felt more comfortable with the idea of dating.

GIRLS, GIRLS, GIRLS

As his videos were racking up hits on YouTube, Justin was navigating his first year of middle school at Stratford Northwestern Public School. He continued to play hockey and was still known as the class clown, often getting in trouble for laughing, dancing through the halls, or humming.

Like other boys his age, he was also beginning to show an interest in girls. He started dating around the age of 13, even though his mom's rule said he couldn't date until he was 16. He had his first kiss around the same time too. It was at a school dance as part of a bet with his friends to see who could kiss a girl first.

||||||||||||||||||||||||||||||||||||||||||||||||||||||||

TAKING TO THE STREETS

Soon after his Stratford Star appearance, Justin decided he needed a way to raise money to go golfing with his friends. Busking, or singing on the street, is common in Canada, and Justin decided to give it a try. With his mom and grandpa taking turns keeping watch from the car across the street, Justin took up a spot on the steps of Stratford's

Justin earned money busking in Stratford, Ontario.

Avon Theater. Then he pulled out his guitar, set his case in front of him, and began singing. He had hoped to earn $20 a day. Instead, he was surprised to find he made closer to $200 each time he sang.

ENTER SCOOTER BRAUN

By this time, Justin's mom had begun receiving calls from agents and managers who had seen Justin's YouTube videos and wanted to represent

Scooter Braun was only 25 years old when he discovered Justin's videos on YouTube. Two years earlier, he had left his position as marketing director at the record label So So Def Recordings to start his own business managing artists. Braun's goal was to discover three specific new artists: the next white rapper, an all-female group, and a youngster who "could do it like Michael Jackson—sing songs that adults would appreciate and be reminded of the innocence they once felt about love."[4] He had already signed white rapper Asher Roth. Now he planned to make Justin his new Michael Jackson.

him. But without a lawyer, Pattie was reluctant to pursue any offers, especially since she feared many were scams.

Meanwhile, in Atlanta, Georgia, talent agent Scott "Scooter" Braun had accidentally clicked on a clip of Justin singing "Respect" while looking for another artist's video. What he saw amazed him. "My gut was going crazy," Braun said, "so I tracked him down."[3] Pattie intended to tell Braun to leave them alone, but to her surprise, he won her over. Pattie and Justin agreed to let Braun fly them to Atlanta to see what he had to offer.

In June 2007, Justin and Pattie hopped a plane to Atlanta, where Braun picked them up and drove them to the studio of record producer Jermaine Dupri. As Braun pulled into the parking lot, Justin spotted a black Range Rover and was astounded to see Usher step out of it. Unable to curb his enthusiasm, Justin rushed up to the multiplatinum recording artist and offered to sing something for him. Usher politely declined.

After a few days in Atlanta, Justin and his mom decided to sign a management deal with Braun.

THE FIRST MILLION

In late 2007, Justin's mom recorded him singing "With You" by Chris Brown. Before uploading the video, Pattie sent it to Braun to get his input. Braun liked what he heard—but not what he saw. He texted Pattie that the song was good, but that they should reshoot it once Justin's hair had grown out from the bad haircut he had received the day before. Pattie didn't get the entire message though. She thought Braun had given the green light to upload the video, so she did. When Braun realized what had happened, he was ready to take down the video. But by then, it had already been viewed 25,000 times. He decided to leave well enough alone. Less than a month later, the video hit 1 million views. Justin was ecstatic, as he recalled in his memoir: "Now they all hit a million almost immediately, and I can't tell you how grateful I am, but that first one—that was incredibly thrilling."[5]

Braun sensed Bieber had what it took to become a huge pop star.

Then they went back to Stratford, where they spent the next six months filming more videos for YouTube. Braun's plan was to keep the videos simple and homemade looking so they would retain the feel of Justin's first clips. He was counting on Justin's growing fan base to spread the word about Justin's talent. As he explained, "We'll give it to the kids, let them do the work, so that they feel like it's theirs."[6] And it worked. Soon, Justin's videos had more than a million views.

|||||||||||||||||||||||||||||||||||||||||||||||||||||||||||

REJECTION

During this time, Justin and his mother traveled back to Atlanta a number of times for meetings Braun had arranged with record labels. But everywhere they went, Justin was turned down. The record labels believed that in order for a teen star to succeed, he had to be familiar to his audience already. And that meant starring in a television show linked to the Disney Channel or Nickelodeon. Although Braun insisted Justin already had a huge following on YouTube, the record labels were not interested. No artist had ever been launched based on YouTube views, and they were not about to take a risk on this one.

||||||||||

Usher acted as a mentor and comanager for Justin when the young singer was trying to get noticed by record labels.

CHAPTER 4

Beginning of the Dream

||||||||||||||||||||||||||||||||||||||||||||||||||||||||||||||||||

With the record label meetings going nowhere, Braun decided Justin needed the backing of an experienced singer to get the labels' attention. He turned to two artists who had gotten their starts in the music business as teenagers: Usher and Justin Timberlake. Justin sang for both stars—and both liked what they heard. "He had all the nuances of a classic artist," Usher said.

"Very cute, for all the young girls—gotta have that. He had swagger. And most important, he had talent."[1] A bidding war ensued between Usher and Timberlake. In the end, Usher put in the better offer, and Justin decided to go with him. Braun and Usher formed a partnership known as the Raymond Braun Media Group to manage Justin's career.

Usher immediately took Justin to Antonio "L. A." Reid, chief executive officer of Island Def Jam Music Group. (Reid resigned in 2011 to serve

A MENTOR AND FRIEND

One of the reasons Braun introduced Justin to Usher was because he felt Usher could help Justin navigate the difficulties of becoming a teen star, since Usher himself had entered the music business at age 14. For his part, Usher was eager to serve as a mentor for Justin. "I knew what pitfalls were out there and how to help him avoid them," Usher said. "I think the best advice I could give him was to stay humble through the whole experience."[2] In addition to serving as Justin's mentor, Usher has also been a friend and a big brother figure for the young singer. "Sometimes he's like a little brother or a son to me," Usher said of Justin.[3] Justin appreciates the time he gets to spend with Usher. "We just hang out and don't really talk about music a lot. We go go-karting and to arcades and movies," he reported of their relationship.[4]

as a judge on the televised singing competition *The X Factor*). Reid had given Usher his start, and Usher thought he would be the guy to get Justin going in the recording industry. In April 2008, Justin, his mother, Braun, and Usher traveled to Reid's office in New York City. Justin sang a couple of songs for Reid. The executive called a few more people into the room, and Justin sang for them too. And then the meeting was over.

Justin and his mom went back to Stratford, where Justin returned to his everyday life while waiting to hear from Braun. Finally, the call came: Reid wanted to sign him.

||||||||||||||||||||||||||||||||||||||||||||||||||||||||||||

THE BIG MOVE

With a record deal in the making, Justin and his mom made plans for a permanent move to Atlanta. They sold all of their furniture and took up residence with Justin's grandparents for the summer. Then they waited for the necessary paperwork to be completed for their move to the United States. Justin once again spent his summer busking in front of the Avon Theatre. In the fall, Justin started ninth grade at Northwestern

Secondary School. Finally, it was time to go. Justin said good-bye to his grandparents and his friends, and he and his mom headed for their new life, bringing only their clothes and Justin's guitar with them.

Justin and his mom moved into a house Braun had found for them. Justin didn't get into the studio right away, but he did get busy with schoolwork. Since he would soon be spending much of his time recording and promoting his music, Justin began working with a tutor from the School of Young Performers. He also took lessons with Usher's voice coach, Jan Smith, whom everyone called Mama Jan.

|||||||||||||||||||||||||||||||||||||||||||||||||

PERFORMING FOR THE STARS ||||||||||||||||||||||||||||||||||||||||||||||||

Justin's voice coach, Mama Jan, usually took on only top artists, but she accepted Justin at Usher's prompting. Shortly after Justin began working with Mama Jan, she held a show at Eddie's Attic, a famed music venue near Atlanta. Justin was thrilled to be invited to sing. At the end of his performance of his original song, "Common Denominator," he was even more thrilled when the major artists who had been with Mama Jan for years gave him a standing ovation.

Jan Smith was the vocal coach for Usher and Justin.

IN THE STUDIO

It was finally time to start recording. Reid and Usher brought in top R&B and pop songwriters such as Christopher "Tricky" Stewart, Terius "The-Dream" Nash, and Kuk Harrell to develop original music for the new artist. As Justin recorded his first songs at Atlanta's famous Triangle Sound Studios, he found he loved the work. He even had an opportunity to offer ideas for lyrics and music on several songs.

By early 2009, Justin had recorded ten songs, and Braun took them to Reid. Reid was impressed. He was ready to release Justin's first singles.

The plan was to release four singles before Justin's first album even hit the shelves. The first song was released in April 2009. Titled "One Time," it is a fast-paced, upbeat pop and soul number Justin described as "about being in a typical teen relationship."[5] Sales were slow at first, but in June, the music video for the song hit YouTube. The video quickly spread and fueled the debut of "One Time" on the *Billboard* Hot 100, a list of the 100 most popular songs each week, in July. The song started at Number 95 and, over the next six months, climbed to Number 17. "One Time" did even better in Canada, where it reached Number 12.

||||||||||||||||||||||||||||||||||||||||||||||||||||

"ONE TIME" FOR THE FIRST TIME ||||||||||||||||||||||||||||||||||||||||||||

In an interview with Radio Disney's *Total Access*, Justin recalled hearing his single "One Time" on the radio for the first time: "I was in the car and . . . we were changing the channel. All of the sudden I was like, 'What?' I turned back. I was with my mom so we were jamming out and I was like, 'This is very weird.'. . . We listened to it for a couple of seconds and then I changed [the channel]."[6]

L. A. Reid had a huge influence in the music industry. In addition to signing Justin, Reid's label signed Usher, Rihanna, and Kanye West.

BEING SOCIAL

One of the major factors in Justin's early success was his use of social networking sites such as Facebook, MySpace, and Twitter to spread the word about his music. The video for "One Time" was scheduled to be released on a Tuesday morning, but following a big promotional blitz on digital music site iTunes, it was accidentally released two weeks early on a Friday night. No ads for the video had been posted at all. Braun and Justin simply posted a note on Justin's Facebook page and sent out a tweet urging fans to check out the video and spread the word. By Monday morning, "One Time" was the Number 3 video on iTunes.

From then on, social media was a regular part of Justin's career. He was constantly posting messages on Facebook or sending tweets to his fans. He often replied to fan comments or re-tweeted their messages. He frequently let them know where he was, what he was doing, and

BY THE NUMBERS

Since the beginning of his career, Justin has been an avid user of social media, and so have his fans. As of October 2011, Justin had more than 1.3 million YouTube subscribers, more than 1.4 million MySpace friends, more than 13.5 million followers on Twitter, and more than 36.5 million likes on Facebook. All told, his videos had been viewed more than 350 million times on YouTube. He had sent more than 10,000 tweets and was ranked Number 2 (after Lady Gaga but before US President Barack Obama) on a list of the most followed people on Twitter.

ON THE CHARTS WITH MICHAEL JACKSON

The week after Justin's video for "One Time" was released, pop icon Michael Jackson died. As a result, Jackson's songs and videos immediately shot to the top of sales charts on iTunes, knocking many hits by current artists off. Justin's "One Time" single went to Number 14 on iTunes, where it had been Number 2. The video, however, remained in the top ten, along with Jackson's videos. Justin said it was a strange experience to be included on the charts with one of his biggest idols.

even how he was feeling. As a result, fans felt like they really knew the emerging celebrity, and they became loyal followers.

||||||||||

Justin went to work promoting his single in 2009. He did interviews at radio and TV stations all over the United States.

CHAPTER 5

Hitting the Road

||||||||||||||||||||||||||||||||||||||||||||||||

Though Justin's first single did well on iTunes and YouTube, his team was disappointed to find that radio stations were slow to pick it up. They decided they would have to go to "every radio station on Planet Earth," according to Justin, to promote the song.[1] So even though Justin and his mom were still getting used to life in Atlanta—and Justin was seeing a girl there—they packed their bags and hit the

DEALING WITH CLAUSTROPHOBIA

When Justin was younger, he was once trapped in an elevator for four hours. As a result, he became very claustrophobic. His claustrophobia sometimes made it hard to deal with fans mobbing him. "It's very definitely scary when girls are all around me and I can't go anywhere. At the same time, I guess I got to get used to it," he said in a 2009 interview.[2]

road in May 2009. From then on, traveling would be Justin's new life. Wherever he went, he would get up early to do radio station and television interviews, perform at malls or amusement parks, or make appearances at stores. At first, the crowds were small, but soon Justin started tweeting to let his fans know where he would be, and huge crowds began following him wherever he went.

On June 20, Justin made his first big concert appearance—a live performance of "One Time" at the Sandstone Amphitheater in Kansas. Dancers were hired for the show, and they became part of Justin's entourage, along with his mom, Braun, and stylist Ryan Good. By August 28, Justin was ready for an even bigger performance. He took part in the MTV Video Music Awards (VMAs) Tour for its show at Six Flags Magic Mountain in Jackson,

New Jersey. Instead of his usual one- or two-song performance, Justin performed four songs there and was met with wild cheers from the huge crowd that had gathered despite the rain.

In September, the extent of Justin's growing popularity was evident when he appeared at the Nintendo World Store in New York City. The night before Justin's September 1 appearance, hundreds of girls and their parents set up camp around the store. By the next morning, approximately 2,000

IN STYLE

Early in Justin's career, Braun brought in Ryan Good to serve as the new star's stylist and "swagger coach."[3] According to Justin, Good helped him stay "swaggerific," which he defined as exhibiting confidence and style.[4] Good definitely made a mark on Justin's wardrobe early on. The stylist reported that when he picked up Justin for his first concert, the boy was wearing a suit. Good quickly changed Justin's style, leading the singer to perform in sweatshirts, white denim, or black stocking caps.

And Justin soon discovered he loved shoes. He could often be found in high-tops ranging in color from bright blue to yellow, red, or purple. When asked to describe his style, Justin was at a loss: "I don't really know, I can't really describe it. I just think it looks good, that's all."[5] With his new interest in fashion, Justin did not rule out the possibility of developing a clothing line at some point in the future.

girls had gathered. Only 150 were allowed into the store for his performance, but not wanting to disappoint his fans outside, Justin waved and blew kisses to them from a window.

||||||||||||||||||||||||||||||||||||||||||||||||||||

PLAYING DEFENSE

Also in September, Justin's mark on the music world was recognized when he was asked to be a presenter at the VMAs. Before the awards show, Justin was ecstatic to meet some of his favorite artists. Moments before Justin took the stage to introduce a live performance by Taylor Swift, the audience was shocked by the antics of rapper Kanye West.

West jumped onstage during Swift's acceptance speech for best music video, grabbed the microphone, and said the award should have gone to Beyoncé. Before Justin began his scripted presentation, he said, "Give it up for Taylor Swift. She *deserved* that award!"[6] Justin's defense of the 19-year-old country singer led to a longstanding friendship between the two.

||||||||||||||||||||||||||||||||||||||||||||||||||||

MORE SINGLES HIT THE CHARTS

A couple of weeks after the scandalous 2009 VMAs, Justin's second single, "One Less Lonely Girl," was released on October 6. The song reached 113,000 downloads on iTunes in its first week. Such sales fueled a rise to Number 16 on the *Billboard* charts.

Justin's third single, "Love Me," was released on October 26 and reached Number 37 on the charts. Approximately a week later, the single "Favorite Girl" debuted at Number 26. The success of Justin's first four singles set a record: he was the first solo artist to ever have four singles from a debut album chart in the top 40 before the album's release.

||||||||||||||||||||||||||||||||||||||||||||||||||

"ONE LESS LONELY GIRL" ||||||||||||||||||||||||||||||||||||||||||||||||||

The video for Justin's single "One Less Lonely Girl" shows the singer smiling at a beautiful girl in a Laundromat. When the girl drops her scarf, Justin creates a treasure hunt to lead her to it—and to him. To give the video a small-town feel, Justin and his crew traveled to Watertown, Tennessee, for filming. Justin's mother was even convinced to appear in a brief cameo in the film. She sits at a table near a florist's cart and smiles at the girl as she passes by on her quest.

As his singles moved up the charts, Justin's fan base continued growing.

LIFE ON THE ROAD

While his new songs were hitting the charts, Justin continued his exhausting promotional tour.

On October 12, Justin appeared on NBC's *Today* show. The show regularly hosts concerts in Rockefeller Plaza outside its studios, and these concerts usually draw large crowds. But none of the performers that year drew as large a crowd as Justin, who brought in an estimated 2,000 people. Many of them had camped out for two nights before Justin's scheduled performance. Justin also made appearances on *Good Morning America* and *The Ellen DeGeneres Show*, among others.

Justin's schedule was grueling. Each day, he woke up early for three hours of tutoring. Then he made his appearances—often several in one day. On the rare occasions he had downtime, he skateboarded, played video games, or sent out tweets.

JUSTIN, THE ACTOR

In late October 2009, Justin took his first stab at acting, appearing on the Nickelodeon comedy *True Jackson, VP*. In the episode, the show's main character, True, is trying to raise money for her school's design department but can't find a performer for her fund-raising concert. Justin, playing himself, comes to the rescue by offering to sing in the concert. Unfortunately, he is injured and can't go on, and three school band members must save the show.

Justin's crew tried to make sure he had at least one day a week off to relax. Sometimes his friends Ryan and Chaz were flown in from Stratford to visit. The boys would do "normal" teenage boy stuff—play soccer or basketball, watch movies, or play video games. Justin credited his friends with helping him stay "just Justin":

> When we're hanging out and I say something stupid or something, they're not going to treat me like I'm a superstar, by any means. . . . They're going to pop me in the head and not care.[7]

Like any teenager, Justin also had moments of rebellion. Sometimes, if he was tired of being around his mom and his bodyguards, he would charge ahead of them through hotel lobbies. Although frustrated, his mother understood. "No 15-year-old wants to be around his mother 24/7," she said.[8] But similar to other 15-year-olds, Justin

KEEPING HIS CHILDHOOD

Even as he was growing up quickly, Justin wanted to make sure he would have a chance to be a regular kid. As he and Braun listened to a speech in which Madonna said the world had taken away Michael Jackson's childhood, Justin turned to look at Braun and said, "Don't let that happen to me," Braun recalled.[9]

Even though he loved performing for his fans, Justin enjoyed being a regular kid whenever he had the chance.

also had to face the consequences of such actions, which often meant the loss of his cell phone or computer.

|||||||||

Justin's first album, *My World*, was an instant hit all over the world.

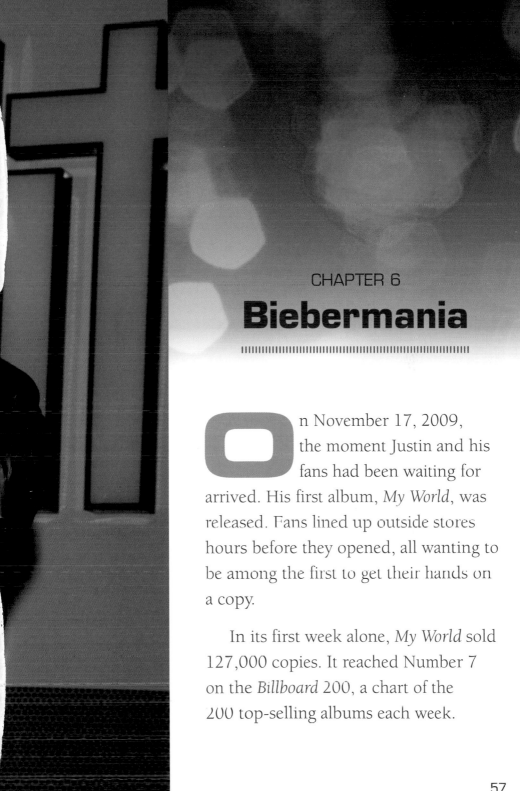

CHAPTER 6

Biebermania

||||||||||||||||||||||||||||||||||||||||||||||||||||||||||||||||||||||||||||

On November 17, 2009, the moment Justin and his fans had been waiting for arrived. His first album, *My World*, was released. Fans lined up outside stores hours before they opened, all wanting to be among the first to get their hands on a copy.

In its first week alone, *My World* sold 127,000 copies. It reached Number 7 on the *Billboard* 200, a chart of the 200 top-selling albums each week.

The album reached Number 1 on the Canadian charts and appeared in the top 40 in a number of other countries, including the United Kingdom, Germany, and Mexico. Within a month, *My World* had gone gold, and it was certified platinum in January 2010.

||||||||||||||||||||||||||||||||||||||||||||||||||||

BIEBER FEVER

After the release of his album, Justin continued to make appearances across the continent, and the crowds that flocked to see him became even larger—and often unruly. On November 20, 2009, Justin was scheduled to appear at the Roosevelt Field Mall in Garden City, New York. Young girls and their parents began arriving at the mall early in the morning, even though Justin was not scheduled to appear until 4:00 p.m. Eventually, thousands of fans showed up.

A couple of hours before Justin was due to arrive, girls began shouting out false alarms that they had spotted the singer. The crowd surged forward. Many fans were knocked to the ground, and a few were injured. Deciding the situation was becoming dangerous, police canceled the event and

GIRLS LOVE HIM

As Biebermania swept the world, it was clear young girls everywhere loved the rising star. They would wait for hours—or even camp overnight—just for a glimpse of him. Rain would not keep them away. Even police barricades couldn't hold them back. But what, exactly, did they love about him? "He's so sweet. He's not like every other guy who is just like, 'Ugh, whatever,'" explained one fan.[1] Another loved Justin because, she reported, "He's not like any other singer. He has a heart."[2] Other fans said they liked Justin's hair, which until 2011 he wore in a sideswept "swoosh," his smile, and his laugh.

Reid summed up Justin's attraction to the opposite sex: "The girls . . . think he's their boyfriend, that there's a shot for them. Justin sold them a dream, and they are buying it hook, line, and sinker."[3]

ordered Justin's crew to send out tweets asking the fans to disperse. Although tweets were eventually sent, police did not feel Justin's team acted quickly enough. As a result, James Roppo, an executive at Island Def Jam, was arrested. Charges were later brought against Braun as well. All charges were dropped in 2011.

For his part, Justin felt terrible that his fans had been let down. "It was crazy and a bit unfair,"

Even as Justin was rising to become one of the most popular teen stars on the planet, he had his share of detractors, or "haters." Several "I hate Justin Bieber" pages were started on Facebook. Some software companies even created programs that would block Internet browsers from displaying any mention of the singer.

Other attacks on the singer were more vicious. Some people sent Internet messages claiming Justin was dead. Hackers redirected his YouTube address to adult sites. And haters even spread rumors that his mother was going to pose for *Playboy*, an adult magazine that features sexual images. For the most part, Justin tried to ignore such antics: "If you just dwell on the negativity it will drag you down."[5] Once in a while, though, he showed his frustration, as in this Twitter post, "Why would people take time out from their day to hate on a sixteen-year-old?"[6]

he told a television interviewer. "It's Biebermania. What can I say?"[4]

BREAK A LEG

Justin's busy schedule included overseas stops as well. On November 23, 2009, he was in London to open for a Taylor Swift concert at Wembley Arena. With 12,000 fans in the audience, this was

Justin's biggest performance to date. And it was going well—until he got to his next-to-last song, "One Time." As he came down the ramp onto the stage, Justin rolled his foot and felt pain instantly shoot from his toes up to his neck. Fighting the urge to scream, Justin finished the song and waved to his fans before limping backstage. Once there, he finally let his pain show, howling and crying as paramedics were called. Justin was whisked off to the hospital, where he discovered his foot was broken.

Two nights later, Justin was scheduled to open for Swift again, this time in Manchester. He decided he was not going to let a foot in a cast stop him. Instead of performing his usual upbeat dance moves, Justin sat on a stool for his entire set. Afterward, he was rewarded with a standing ovation.

||||||||||||||||||||||||||||||||||||||||||||||||||||||

A BUSY CHRISTMAS

After the concerts with Swift, Justin made a brief tour through Europe to promote both *My World* and his upcoming second album, *My World 2.0*, which would be released in March 2010. Then it was back to the United States to perform at the Z100 Jingle Ball at Madison Square Garden. The Jingle Ball was the biggest holiday music event of the year, and it included a number of big acts, including Taylor Swift and John Mayer. But the loudest screams of the night were reserved for Justin. Although still in a cast, he managed to perform modified versions of some of his dance moves.

The Jingle Ball was only the start of a busy weekend. Immediately after the concert, Justin flew to Las Vegas, Nevada, where he taped a performance for Dick Clark's *New Year's Rockin' Eve*. Then he hopped on a plane to Chicago, Illinois, for another concert.

He ended the weekend in Washington DC with a performance for the annual *Christmas in Washington* television special. Although Justin had repeatedly said performing didn't scare him, this time he admitted he was a bit nervous. After all, he would be singing for President Barack Obama and his wife, Michelle. Justin did not want to appear in front of such an important audience in his cast, so he took it off. And he put on a tie.

A broken foot was not enough to stop Justin from performing.

JUSTIN EVERYWHERE

After taking a short break to celebrate Christmas with his family, Justin was back to work. He served as a presenter at the Grammys on January 31, 2010, and in February, he joined more than 80 famous musicians to record a remake of Michael Jackson's famous song, "We Are the World." Jackson and others originally created the song 25 years earlier to benefit famine relief in Africa. The new version would benefit victims of a devastating earthquake that had rocked Haiti on January 12. Justin was honored to sing the song's opening lines.

Also in February, Justin traveled to Paris, France, where he was met by mobs much larger than the police had anticipated. An event at a store

DOING MORE FOR HAITI

On February 5, 2010, Justin sang at the SOS Saving OurSelves—Help for Haiti benefit concert. Since French is one of the official languages of Haiti, Justin sang the first verse of "One Less Lonely Girl" in French. He also changed the chorus of "Baby" to "baby, baby, Haiti." In addition to singing, Justin also answered phones to take donations— much to the delight of the screaming donors who were lucky enough to have him take their call.

Justin was honored by an invitation to present at the Grammys in 2010, alongside fellow pop star Kesha.

called Citadium had to be canceled early as fans, anxious to see Justin, pushed aside barricades and shoved their way forward.

After the chaos of Paris, Justin was scheduled to make a quiet, unpublicized appearance at radio station Q102 in Philadelphia, Pennsylvania. But the event became loud and very public when Justin sent out a tweet letting fans know when and where he would arrive. The crowd that showed up was wild. As Justin tried to get back to his van after his interview, girls grabbed at his hair, his arms—whatever they could reach. Even when his security guards managed to get Justin back into the van, girls began pounding on the vehicle, rocking it back and forth.

Memories of such scenes led Justin's security team to be more cautious after that. If a large, unruly group gathered outside an event, they would sometimes insist on smuggling Justin out a side door. Knowing his fans would be disappointed

A DAY IN JUSTIN'S LIFE ||||||||||||||||||||||||||||||||||||||||||||||||||||||||||||||||

The MTV special *Diary of Justin Bieber* followed a day in the star's life while he was in Paris. Among other things, the special revealed that Justin has a hard time getting up in the morning, likes jumping on the bed, and considers many of his team members like big brothers. It also showed that Justin's mom is not afraid to discipline her famous son and make him apologize for inappropriate remarks.

Wherever Justin went, a mob of fans followed.

with such actions, Justin would send a tweet apologizing and explaining why he had not been able to meet with them. As always, he knew it was important to keep his fans happy.

||||||||||

By his sixteenth birthday, Justin was already a chart-topping artist.

CHAPTER 7
Sweet Sixteen

||||||||||||||||||||||||||||||||||||||||||||||||||||||||||||||||||||||||||||||||||||||

As he approached his sixteenth birthday, Justin had already sold millions of albums and reached the top of the charts in 17 countries. Such success meant he had the means to throw an elaborate birthday bash. For his three-day celebration, Justin invited friends and important figures from the music industry to Los Angeles. There, he treated them to a huge birthday dinner on February 27. The next day, guests were invited to a private screening of the new movie *The Book of Eli*. And on March 1—Justin's actual birthday—guests enjoyed swimming, karaoke, sumo wrestling, laser tag, and basketball. As for gifts, Usher topped them all when he gave Justin a Range Rover.

After his big party, Justin flew to Canada, where he celebrated with family and friends. Though not quite as lavish a party—they went bowling— Justin enjoyed the opportunity to be around people who had known and loved him before he became famous.

|||||||||||||||||||||||||||||||||||||||||||||||||||

GROWING UP

Now that he was 16, Justin's mother allowed him to officially begin dating. Although the star was private about his love life, rumors began flying. Among the girls reported at one time or another to be in a relationship with Justin were dancer Jaquelle, actress Elissa Sursara, and singer Taylor Swift.

Like any 16-year-old, Justin was also eager to get his driver's license. Although his busy promotional schedule made it difficult to find time to practice driving, Justin's dad gave him lessons whenever he could join Justin on the road or when the two found time to get together in Canada. The big day finally came, and Justin texted everyone that he would be getting his license. But Justin hadn't studied for the test, and he failed it by one question. He had to wait 30 days to try again. Finally, on April 13, Justin walked out of the department of motor vehicles with his license.

SCREAMING AT THE WORLD

Justin was usually calm and mild-mannered, but after he failed his driver's test, he was disappointed and angry. When he and his mom walked out of the testing site, Justin pulled on his hood and sunglasses and sulked toward the car. But when his mom got in the driver's seat—the seat he had been planning on taking until he failed his test—Justin couldn't take it. He started walking, despite the fact that it was raining.

Then he started yelling at the cars going past. Although his mom followed in the car and occasionally pleaded with him to get in, she waited patiently until he was done.

Justin may have felt a little better after his rant, but his voice did not. The next day, he could barely talk. He was put on strict voice rest, and Braun had to cancel his upcoming engagements.

While dating and driving affected only Justin's personal life, another part of turning 16 affected his professional life as well. Sometime around his birthday, Justin noticed his voice was beginning to crack. Suddenly, it was becoming difficult to hit high notes. As a result, he had to lower the key of some songs, including "Baby." Justin didn't try to hide his struggles but assured his fans that he was working with his vocal coach and he would get through it.

MY WORLD 2.0

Meanwhile, Justin kept up his busy promotional tour, appearing in Germany and the United Kingdom in March. By now, he had been on the road almost constantly for ten months. In between promotional spots during those busy months, he still managed to find some time in the studio to record his next album, *My World 2.0*. "Baby," the first single from that album, had been released on January 18. The song, which includes a rap from hip-hop star Ludacris, became another instant hit, reaching Number 5 on the *Billboard* Hot 100.

As Justin matured, he had to make changes to some of his songs to work with his changing voice.

The day after Justin's sixteenth birthday, the album's second single, "Never Let You Go," was released. Two weeks later, fans were treated to "U Smile," a song Justin said he cowrote especially for "all my fans who got me here. U took me from a small town in Canada to this amazing opportunity I am living now."[1]

On March 19, *My World 2.0* hit stores. Just as they had with Justin's first album, fans lined up hours ahead of time to make sure they would get their copy. The album debuted at Number 1 on the *Billboard* 200, making Justin the youngest solo male artist to top the chart since Stevie Wonder in 1963. By May, the album had gone platinum, and in September, it was certified double platinum, selling more than 2 million copies.

||||||||||||||||||||||||||||||||||||||||||||||||||

GOING NONSTOP

Even after his album was released, Justin continued his promotional tour, appearing on late-night

BRINGING IN THE LAUGHS

For his *Saturday Night Live* appearance, Justin was originally scheduled to simply sing. But when he was offered the opportunity to appear in a couple of skits as well, he jumped at it. In one sketch, he appeared with *Saturday Night Live* veteran Tina Fey, who played a high school teacher with a crush on her student—played by Justin. Throughout the skit, Justin sweet talks Fey, smiles at her, and sings to her. Most reviews of Justin's performance were positive.

Justin is known for his appreciation of his fans and his willingness to connect with them through social media or meet and greets.

talk shows with David Letterman and Jay Leno. He returned to Washington DC to perform at the White House for the annual Easter Egg Roll on April 5. He was also the musical guest on *Saturday Night Live* and sat for interviews with news outlets such as *Nightline* and the *CBS Evening News*.

On April 18, Justin traveled to Canada to perform at the Juno Awards, the Canadian equivalent of the Grammys. Although he had been nominated for three awards—Album of the Year, Pop Album of the Year, and New Artist of the Year—he failed to take any home. After the awards show, he was off to Japan and then to Australia. In a repeat of his experiences in Garden City and Paris, a scheduled concert in Sydney was canceled after the crowd of 4,000 became unruly.

From Australia, Justin flew to New Zealand, where he found the crowds were even crazier. When he landed at the airport, 500 girls were there to greet him, and some managed to push past security. One girl stole the hat off Justin's head and ran away. Others knocked his mother down. Justin

JEALOUS FANS

Justin's fans are a jealous group. The singer learned the extent of their jealousy when he tweeted a picture of himself with reality television star Kim Kardashian. He joked that the picture was of his girlfriend. Justin's fans immediately began to post online threats to Kardashian. The uproar became so great that Kardashian had to ask Justin to make them stop. He did so by tweeting that Kardashian was just a friend.

BREAKING COLOR BARRIERS

In May 2010, Black Entertainment Television (BET) announced Justin had been nominated for a BET Award for Best New Artist. Although the awards program traditionally honors only black performers, an exception was made for Justin. "Bieber has crossed the color boundaries," Stephen Hill, BET's president of music programming and specials, said. "He's had rhythm in his music. He makes the kind of music our audience likes."[3] Justin lost the award to Nicki Minaj.

was not pleased. He sent out a tweet: "The airport was crazy. Not happy that someone stole my hat and knocked down my mama. Come on people."[2] Before leaving the country, Justin managed to find some time to go bungee jumping.

Things calmed down a bit when Justin returned to the United States, but he was still plenty busy. In May, he appeared on *Oprah*, threw the first pitch at a Chicago White Sox game, sang on *American Idol*, and performed at Wango Tango, a concert in Los Angeles featuring numerous stars. In June, he again appeared on the *Today* show before performing at a private concert in the Bahamas. In between such appearances, Justin was getting ready for his next big venture—his first headlining tour.

||||||||||

Justin headlined his first tour,
the My World Tour, in 2010.

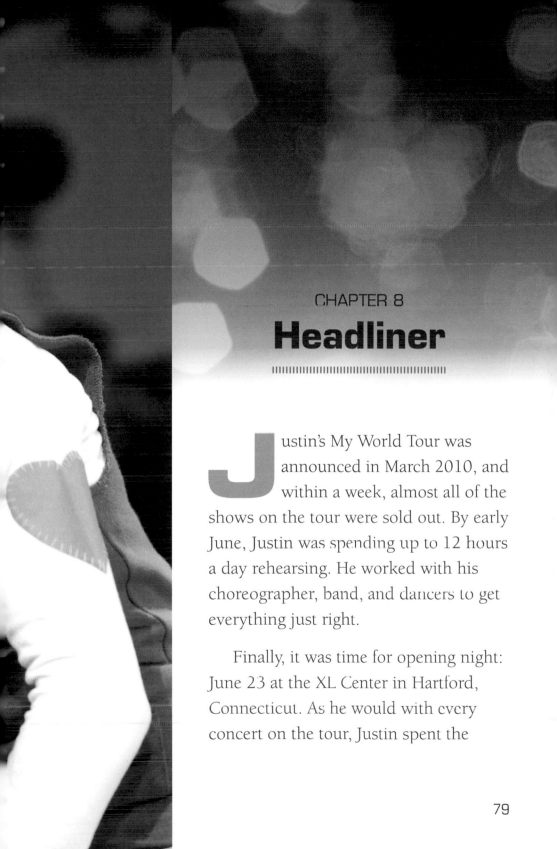

CHAPTER 8

Headliner

||||||||||||||||||||||||||||||||||||||||||||||||||

Justin's My World Tour was announced in March 2010, and within a week, almost all of the shows on the tour were sold out. By early June, Justin was spending up to 12 hours a day rehearsing. He worked with his choreographer, band, and dancers to get everything just right.

Finally, it was time for opening night: June 23 at the XL Center in Hartford, Connecticut. As he would with every concert on the tour, Justin spent the preshow hours at a special event for approximately 200 fans who had paid $350 to get close to their heartthrob. He answered the girls' questions, ran through a song, and then posed for pictures with each girl. As the time for the concert approached, Justin warmed up with his vocal coach. Then he and his crew prayed together.

And then Justin was on. As he started singing, his voice was almost drowned out by the thousands of screaming fans. But Justin didn't mind the noise. He loved performing live, and he loved the chance to interact with his fans. During several songs, he walked to the edge of the stage, reaching out to touch the hands stretched toward him. He flew above the crowd in a metal hot-air balloon basket. He danced. And he talked to his fans, deciding what to say as he went along. This was the one part of the show he never practiced ahead of time. He wanted to be able to say what he was feeling as he looked out at the crowd.

After his performance at the XL Center, Justin and his crew packed up their 12 buses and ten semis and hit the road for the next night's concert in Trenton, New Jersey. Then it was on to Cincinnati, Ohio. Before the end of the month, he

Although Justin was obviously the star of the show, he was not the only performer onstage during his concerts. His band members and backup dancers helped make each performance a success, and Justin made it a point to recognize each of them during the show. With Michael Jackson's "Wanna Be Startin' Somethin'" in the background, Justin showcased each band member and dancer individually. Justin thought of it as a way to let the members of his music family have their moment in the spotlight too.

had also put on shows in Milwaukee, Wisconsin; Minneapolis, Minnesota; and Des Moines, Iowa. Justin's grueling schedule continued. By Christmas, he had traveled across the United States and Canada to perform 76 concerts in six months.

||||||||||||||||||||||||||||||||||||||||||||||||||||

ALWAYS GOING

The My World Tour was not the only thing on Justin's plate, though. In between concerts, he continued to make appearances around North America. In September 2010, he appeared at the VMAs at the Nokia Theater in Los Angeles. There, he performed three songs and went home with the Best New Artist award. That month, Justin also had a spot in the season premiere of the CBS crime drama *CSI*, playing a teenager who becomes a terrorist. Actress Marg Helgenberger, who worked with Justin on the set, later called Justin a brat for locking a producer in a closet.

In October, Justin published a photo memoir titled *Justin Bieber: First Step 2 Forever: My Story*. A chronicle of his early life and discovery, the book was an instant bestseller. Justin helped promote it with book signings in New York and elsewhere.

At the American Music Awards on November 21, Justin picked up four awards: Artist of the Year: Pop/Rock Music; Favorite Male Artist: Pop/Rock Music; Favorite Album: *My World 2.0*; and T-Mobile Breakthrough Artist of the Year. In his acceptance speech, Justin paid tribute to his idol, saying, "I want to thank Michael Jackson, because without Michael Jackson, none of us would be here."[1]

Two days later, Justin released his third album, *My Worlds Acoustic*, featuring acoustic versions of several songs from his previous two albums along with the new track, "Pray." Justin said the purpose of the album was to show he really could sing. "There's a lot with production, it kind of drowns

Justin shows off his American Music Awards.

Even as his own career skyrocketed, Justin felt it was important to support young talent. Returning to Stratford in the middle of his My World Tour, Justin stopped to listen to a young girl playing violin outside the Avon Theatre. He told her he had played there too, and he encouraged her to follow her dreams.

out your voice," he said, "and it takes away from the singer."[2]

PUTTING HIS NAME ON IT

Even as he continued his concert tour, promoted his book and new album, and made appearances at awards shows, Justin also found time for a number of promotional deals. In addition to videos endorsing Proactiv acne cream and JustBeats headphones, Justin also began to offer his own product lines. In November, he released a series of fragrance-infused dog tags and wristbands featuring his picture. Then, in December, the "One Less Lonely Girl" nail polish line hit shelves, featuring shades with names like "Baby" Blue and "One Time" Lime. Among the must-have presents for Justin fans that Christmas were Justin Bieber

In front of Stratford's Avon Theater, Justin encourages a young violinist to pursue her dreams.

dolls. The dolls came in five versions, each wearing different styles, and two versions even sang.

With such promotions, Justin ended the year on a high note. Polls showed he had become the most recognized celebrity among teens. His *My World 2.0* album was the fourth-highest selling album of the year. His tour was ranked Number 10 for the year, bringing in more than $48 million in sales.

||||||||||

Justin Bieber and girlfriend
Selena Gomez were an official
couple in early 2011.

CHAPTER 9

Keeping It Going

||||||||||||||||||||||||||||||||

Justin spent New Year's weekend of 2011 on the Caribbean island of Saint Lucia. But he was not alone. The paparazzi managed to snag photographs of Justin with 18-year-old Selena Gomez, popular star of the Disney Channel show *Wizards of Waverly Place* and lead singer of the band Selena Gomez & the Scene. The two had been friends for several years, and rumors of their closer relationship had begun to surface in late 2010. They officially announced they were a couple at a party following the Oscars in late February.

|||||||||||||||||||||||||||||||||||||||||||||||||||||||

WIN SOME, LOSE SOME

Although the North American leg of Justin's tour had wrapped up, fans could still get plenty of the star as *Justin Bieber: Never Say Never* hit theaters on February 11. The 3-D documentary had been filmed in the days before his concert at Madison Square Garden in August 2010. It presents his experience getting ready and performing there, along with an overview of Justin's early life and his rise to fame, with a number of home videos and early YouTube clips. Justin said he wanted the video to show "that I'm not just some product, that I'm just a regular person, and I've been a musician my whole life."[1] The movie was a success, earning $30 million in its first weekend at the box office.

On February 13, Justin was once again invited to the Grammys, this time as a performer and a nominee. Although he was in the running for Best Pop Vocal Album and Best New Artist, Justin won neither award. He was beaten by Lady Gaga

Justin's quick rise to fame also brought him a quick rise in fortune. In 2010 alone, he earned an estimated $53 million. Despite his newfound wealth, Justin insisted he didn't care much about money: "I don't love money, because once you start loving money, you've got a big house and nice cars and just an empty heart."[2]

for Best Pop Vocal Album, and little-known jazz musician, Esperanza Spalding, took home Best New Artist. Afterward, Spalding faced tweeted death threats from Justin's angry fans. Days after the Grammys, Justin fared better at the thirty-first annual Brit Awards in London, where he won International Breakthrough Act.

|||||||||||||||||||||||||||||||||||||||||||||||||||||

GIVING BACK

From the beginning of his career, Justin had been dedicated to giving a portion of his proceeds to charity. During the My World Tour, one dollar of every ticket sold was given to Pencils of Promise, a charity that builds schools in developing countries. A portion of the proceeds from Justin's nail polish line went to charity as well.

After getting his characteristic "swoosh" hairdo cut in February 2011, Justin donated the clippings to a charity auction. They brought in more than $40,000. The next month, after a massive earthquake and tsunami rocked Japan, Justin rerecorded his song "Pray" on a benefit album to raise funds for quake victims.

In June, Justin launched Someday, a fragrance for women. The perfume was expected to raise more than $30 million, with all proceeds going to charities such as Pencils of Promise and the Make-A-Wish Foundation. For Justin, donating to charity was not just about giving back; it was also about moving others to do the same: "It's about encouraging young people to help other young people. I try to motivate my fans to make a difference as much as they can," he said.[3]

SELECTING A SCENT

Justin's perfume, Someday, doesn't just have his name on it. It also has his input. Justin helped determine the name of the perfume, the design of the bottle, and even the scent. "I know what I like on a girl," he said of his role in helping to determine what his fans would smell like.[4]

GOING INTERNATIONAL

In March 2011, Justin began the international leg of his My World Tour, with performances across Europe, Asia, and Australia throughout the spring. During an April trip to Israel, Justin was frustrated by paparazzi, who followed him even while he was trying to pray at holy sites. Later in April, Justin enjoyed a more relaxing trip to Indonesia, where Selena joined him for some quality time together.

In May, Justin kept his concert dates in earthquake-devastated Japan, despite the fact that a number of other performers had canceled their shows in the country. Many feared the threat of radiation leaks from the country's damaged nuclear reactors. After being assured by several experts that they would be in no danger, Justin and his crew decided the show would go on.

After his performances in Japan, Justin returned stateside to appear at the *Billboard* Music Awards. He took home awards in seven categories: Billboard.com Fan Favorite, Top New Artist, Top Social Artist, Top Streaming Artist, Top Digital Media Artist, Top Pop Album, and Top Streaming Song (video). Celebrating with him was Selena,

Bieber visits Japanese children in the wake of the devastating earthquake.

whom he turned to kiss before stepping up to accept his award for Top New Artist.

|||||||||||||||||||||||||||||||||||||||||||||||

A SHORT BREATHER

After two years of working almost nonstop, Justin decided to take the month of July 2011 off. He spent much of his time resting, hanging out with his friends, and enjoying time with Selena. He explained his need for a break:

I'm still growing up, and when you're working every day, you don't really get a chance to figure out who you are. So with the time off, I'm able to think, pray and just kind of grow up.[5]

By August, Justin was refreshed and back to work, making appearances at the Teen Choice Awards and the VMAs. He came away from both with wins. At the Teen Choice Awards, Justin was presented with Choice Music Male Artist, Choice Male Hottie, Choice Twit (for his use of Twitter), and Choice Male Villain (for his role on *CSI*). Despite rumors the two had split up, Justin and Selena sat together at the show and were spotted kissing. At the VMAs, Justin won Best Male Video for "U Smile."

Also in August, Justin announced he was working on his newest album, a collection of original songs for Christmas. The album includes collaborations with a number of other singers, including Sean Kingston, Taylor Swift, and Boyz II Men. Justin also decided proceeds from the album would be donated to charity.

In late September, Justin again packed his bags, this time bringing the My World Tour to Latin

America with stops in Mexico, Brazil, Argentina, Chile, Peru, and Venezuela before the end of October.

||||||||||||||||||||||||||||||||||||||||||||||||||||||

LOOKING AHEAD

Though Justin remained busy with recording and touring, he also continued his schooling with his tutor. He planned to graduate from high school in 2012 and did not rule out the possibility of going to college at some point in the future.

By mid-2011, Justin was beginning to talk about the possibility of appearing in a feature film as well. There were even rumors he might eventually work on a movie with Ashton Kutcher. Even though he was looking to start a film career, Justin's main focus remained on developing musically. Justin knew he wouldn't appeal to young girls forever, but he hoped to successfully make a transition from "being a . . . teenage heartthrob basically to . . . an adult singer," as he put it.[6]

Whatever happened down the road, Justin would always be remembered as the first singer to move so successfully from YouTube to a mainstream singing career. How it all came about

As he grows from teen pop star to adult musician, Justin's opportunities are only expanding.

still surprises him sometimes. For Justin's loyal fans, it doesn't seem crazy at all. They loved him when they discovered his first homemade videos online. And they will likely continue to love him until he sings his last song, far in the future.

TIMELINE

1994

2007

2007

Justin Drew Bieber is born in Ontario, Canada, on March 1.

Justin enters the Stratford Star singing competition and posts videos of his performance on YouTube.

Justin signs a management agreement with Scooter Braun in June.

2009

2009

2009

One June 20, Justin makes his first big concert appearance at the Sandstone Amphitheater in Kansas.

In September, Justin is a presenter at the VMAs and comes to Taylor Swift's defense after Kanye West's rude remark.

On November 17, Justin's first album, *My World*, is released, selling 127,000 copies in the first week.

2008

In April, Justin sings for Island Def Jam CEO L. A. Reid, who decides to sign him.

2008

Justin and his mother move to Atlanta, Georgia, in the fall.

2009

Justin's first single, "One Time," is released in April.

2009

Justin breaks his foot while performing in London on November 23.

2010

"Baby," the first single from Justin's second album, is released on January 18.

2010

Justin's second album, *My World 2.0*, is released on March 19, debuting at Number 1 on the *Billboard* 200.

TIMELINE

2010

2010

2010

On April 13,
Justin gets his
driver's license.

Justin's My World
Tour opens
on June 23.

On September 12,
Justin performs at
the VMAs and wins
Best New Artist.

2011

2011

2011

The concert
documentary,
*Justin Bieber: Never
Say Never,* arrives
in theaters on
February 11.

On May 17,
Justin refuses to
cancel his concerts
in earthquake-
damaged Japan.

Justin takes home
seven awards at
the Billboard Music
Awards on May 22.

In October,
Justin publishes a
memoir titled *Justin
Bieber: First Step 2
Forever: My Story*.

On November 23,
Justin releases
My Worlds Acoustic,
an album featuring
acoustic versions of
several songs from
his previous albums.

Justin and Selena
Gomez announce
they are a couple
in February.

2011

2011

2011

On June 23,
Justin releases the
perfume Someday,
with all proceeds
going to charity.

Justin wins
Best Male Video
for "U Smile"
at the MTV Video
Music Awards
on August 28.

On September 30,
Justin continues
the My World Tour
in Latin America.

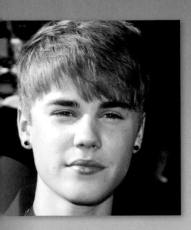

FULL NAME

Justin Drew Bieber

DATE OF BIRTH

March 1, 1994

PLACE OF BIRTH

London, Ontario, Canada

SELECTED ALBUMS

My World (2009), *My World 2.0* (2010), *My Worlds Acoustic* (2010)

FILMS AND SELECTED TELEVISION APPEARANCES

Justin Bieber: Never Say Never (2011), the *Today* show (2009–2011), *American Idol* (2010), *Saturday Night Live* (2010–2011), *CSI: Crime Scene Investigation* (2010–2011)

SELECTED AWARDS

- Won MTV Video Music Award for Best New Artist (2010)
- Won American Music Award for Artist of the Year: Pop/Rock Music (2010)
- Won *Billboard* Music Award for Top New Artist and Top Pop Album (2011)

- Nominated for Grammy Awards for Best Pop Vocal Album and Best New Artist (2011)
- Nominated for Juno Awards for Album of the Year, Pop Album of the Year, and Artist of the Year (2010–2011)

PUBLICATIONS

Justin Bieber: First Step 2 Forever: My Story (2010)

PHILANTHROPY

Justin has supported a number of charitable organizations, including Pencils of Promise and the Make-A-Wish Foundation.

> **"I was once chilling in my room, watching TV, just in a regular place, and now I'm in this big world living my dream and doing what I love and it's just crazy how it all came around."**
>
> *—JUSTIN BIEBER*

GLOSSARY

acoustic—An instrument that is played without the use of electronic devices to enhance its sound.

Billboard—A music chart system used by the music-recording industry to measure record popularity.

chart—A weekly listing of record sales.

choreographer—Someone who creates and arranges the specific movements and steps for a dance.

claustrophobia—Fear of being in small spaces.

collaboration—Working together in order to create or produce a work, such as a song or an album.

debut—A first appearance.

emulate—To imitate someone with the desire to be as good as or better than that person at a specific task.

encore—An additional performance granted at the audience's request after the main performance has concluded.

entourage—One's attendants or associates.

fluent—Able to speak a foreign language smoothly.

gold—A certification for an album that has sold more than 500,000 copies.

headliner—The main act of a show.

hip-hop—A style of popular music associated with US urban culture that features rap spoken against a background of electronic music or beats.

memoir—A literary account of a person's experiences, written by that person.

mentor—A person with experience in a specific field, who guides someone with less experience.

paparazzi—Aggressive photojournalists who take pictures of celebrities and sell them to media outlets.

platinum—A certification for an album that has sold more than 1 million copies.

pyrotechnics—Fireworks and other special effects using explosions.

record label—A brand or trademark related to the marketing of music videos and recordings.

rhythm and blues (R & B)—A kind of music that—especially in modern times—typically combines hip-hop, soul, and funk.

single—An individual song that is distributed on its own over the radio and other mediums.

social media—Internet and cell-phone based technologies that allow users to interact with one another.

studio—A room with electronic recording equipment where music is recorded.

ADDITIONAL RESOURCES

SELECTED BIBLIOGRAPHY

Bieber, Justin. *Justin Bieber: First Step 2 Forever: My Story*. New York: HarperCollins, 2010. Print.

Gatehouse, Jonathon. "A Very Sweet Sixteen." *Maclean's*. 13 Dec. 2010: 86. *MasterFILE Premier*. Ebsco. Web. 13 Aug. 2011.

Grigoriadis, Vanessa. "The Adventure of Super Boy." *Rolling Stone*. 3 March 2011: 52–58. *MAS Ultra-School Edition*. Ebsco. Web. 14 Aug. 2011.

Justin Bieber: Never Say Never. Dir. Jon M. Chu. Perf. Justin Bieber, Pattie Mallette, Scooter Braun. Paramount Home Entertainment, 2011. DVD.

Robinson, Lisa. "The Kid Just Has It." *Vanity Fair*. Feb. 2011: 98–151. *MasterFILE Premier*. Ebsco. Web. 30 Aug. 2011.

FURTHER READINGS

Baldwin, Garrett. *The Justin Bieber Album*. London: Plexus, 2010. Print.

Rowlands, Millie. *Justin Bieber: Our World*. London: Orion, 2010. Print.

WEB SITES

To learn more about Justin Bieber, visit ABDO Publishing Company online at **www.abdopublishing.com**. Web sites about Justin Bieber are featured on our Book Links page. These links are routinely monitored and updated to provide the most current information available.

PLACES TO VISIT

Eddie's Attic
515-B North McDonough Street
Decatur, GA 30030
404-377-4976
http://www.eddiesattic.com
Justin performed at this live music venue shortly after
moving to Atlanta—and got a standing ovation from the
other stars in attendance. The venue continues to offer live
music by performers nearly every night, in addition to a
rooftop grill.

Madame Tussauds Wax Museum
234 West Forty-Second Street
New York, NY 10036
866-841-3505
http://www.madametussauds.com/NewYork/Default.aspx
Fans can catch a lifelike view of Justin at Madame Tussauds.
In 2011, the famous museum unveiled a wax sculpture of
Justin, clothed in an outfit the star himself donated.

Stratford Tourism Alliance
47 Downie Street
Stratford, ON N5A 1W7
800-561-7926
http://www.visitstratford.ca
Stratford offers a "Justin's Stratford" map to guide fans to
his favorite hangouts. Stops include the town's skate park,
various restaurants, Long & McQuade's music store, and the
Avon Theatre.

SOURCE NOTES

CHAPTER 1. CROWD PLEASER

1. Jocelyn Vena. "Justin Bieber Joined by Miley Cyrus, Usher at New York Show." *MTV.* MTV Networks, 1 Sept. 2010. Web. 18 Oct. 2011.

2. Justin Bieber. *Justin Bieber: First Step 2 Forever: My Story.* New York: HarperCollins, 2010. Print. 18.

3. Justin Bieber. "Rescheduled: Justin Bieber Live in Syracuse, NY." *Facebook.* Facebook, 1 Sept. 2010. Web. 1 Sept. 2011.

4. *Justin Bieber: The Untold Story of His Rise to Fame.* Dir. Maureen Goldthorpe. Echo Bridge Home Entertainment, 2011. DVD.

5. "Justin Bieber at Much Music." *YouTube.* YouTube, 14 July 2009. Web. 1 Sept. 2011.

6. Chas Newkey-Burden. *Justin Bieber: The Unauthorized Biography.* London: Michael O'Mara Books, 2010. Print. 217.

CHAPTER 2. YOUNG MUSICIAN

1. *Justin Bieber: Never Say Never.* Dir. Jon M. Chu. Perf. Justin Bieber, Pattie Mallette, Scooter Braun. Paramount Home Entertainment, 2011. DVD.

2. Justin Bieber. *Justin Bieber: First Step 2 Forever: My Story.* New York: HarperCollins, 2010. Print. 42.

3. Nicholas Köhler. "R & B Sensation Justin Bieber on Usher and Justin Timberlake, His Mom and His Fans, and What His Swagger Coach Teaches Him." *Maclean's.* 28 Dec. 2009: 16–17. *MasterFILE Premier.* Ebsco. Web. 19 Aug. 2011.

4. Justin Bieber. *Justin Bieber: First Step 2 Forever: My Story.* New York. HarperCollins, 2010. Print. 52–53.

5. Ibid. 56.

6. *Justin Bieber: A Star Was Born.* Dir. Tex Thomas. Flashlight Entertainment, 2010. DVD.

7. Vanessa Grigoriadis. "The Adventures of Super Boy." *Rolling Stone.* Rolling Stone, 3 March 2011: 52–58. *MAS Ultra-School Edition.* Ebsco. Web. 14 Aug. 2011.

8. Marc Shapiro. *Justin Bieber: The Fever!* New York: St. Martin's Griffin, 2010. Print. 19.

9. Justin Bieber. "Bigger Lyrics." Metrolyrics, 2004–2011. Web. 5 Sept. 2011.

CHAPTER 3. STRATFORD STAR

1. Justin Bieber. *Justin Bieber: First Step 2 Forever: My Story*. New York: HarperCollins, 2010. Print. 87.

2. Ibid. 91.

3. Joey Bartolomeo. "Boy Wonder." *People*. 19 Apr. 2010: 66–72. *Academic Search Premier*. Ebsco. Web. 30 Aug. 2011.

4. Monica Herrera. "Justin Bieber: Young Money." *Billboard*. 27 Mar. 2010: 18–21. *MasterFILE Premier*. Ebsco. Web. 30 Aug. 2011.

5. Justin Bieber. *Justin Bieber: First Step 2 Forever: My Story*. New York: HarperCollins, 2010. Print. 124–125.

6. Jan Hoffman. "Justin Bieber Dream." *New York Times*. 3 Jan. 2010: 1. *Newspaper Source Plus*. Ebsco. Web. 30 Aug. 2011.

CHAPTER 4. BEGINNING OF THE DREAM

1. Jason Gay. "Justin Bieber's Adolescent Fantasy." *Rolling Stone*. 21 Jan. 2010: 22–24. *MasterFILE Premier*. Ebsco. Web. 25 Aug. 2011.

2. Marc Shapiro. *Justin Bieber: The Fever!* New York: St. Martin's Griffin, 2010. Print. 44.

3. Jan Hoffman. "Justin Bieber Dream." *New York Times*. 3 Jan. 2010: 1. *Newspaper Source Plus*. Ebsco. Web. 30 Aug. 2011.

4. Jon Bream. "Bieber Mania!" *Star Tribune*. 5 Dec. 2009. Web. 9 Sept. 2011.

5. Nick Levine. "Justin Bieber." *Digital Spy*. 15 Jan. 2010. Web. 9 Sept. 2011.

6. "Justin Bieber Part 3: Big Moments." *Disney Total Access*. Radio Disney, n.d. Web. 10 Sept. 2011.

CHAPTER 5. HITTING THE ROAD

1. Justin Bieber. *Justin Bieber: First Step 2 Forever: My Story*. New York: HarperCollins, 2010. Print. 178–179.

2. Nicholas Köhler. "R & B Sensation Justin Bieber on Usher and Justin Timberlake, His Mom and His Fans, and What His Swagger Coach Teaches Him." *Maclean's*. 28 Dec. 2009: 16–17. *MasterFILE Premier*. Ebsco. Web. 19

3. Jan Hoffman. "Justin Bieber Dream." *New York Times*. 3 Jan. 2010: 1. *Newspaper Source Plus*. Ebsco. Web. 30 Aug. 2011.

4. Nicholas Köhler. "R & B Sensation Justin Bieber on Usher and Justin Timberlake, His Mom and His Fans, and What His Swagger Coach Teaches Him." *Maclean's*. 28 Dec. 2009: 16–17. *MasterFILE Premier*. Ebsco. Web. 19 Aug. 2011.

5. "Justin Bieber: I Look Good." *Belfast Telegraph*. 9 Sept. 2011. Web. 10 Sept. 2011.

6. Elena Barry. "Taylor Swift Thanks 'Lil Bro' Justin Bieber After Kanye West VMA Tirade!" *Entertainment News Examiner*, 10 Nov. 2009. Web. 10 Sept. 2011.

7. Nicholas Köhler. "R & B Sensation Justin Bieber on Usher and Justin Timberlake, His Mom and His Fans, and What His Swagger Coach Teaches Him." *Maclean's*. 28 Dec. 2009: 16–17. *MasterFILE Premier*. Ebsco. Web. 19 Aug. 2011.

8. Jan Hoffman. "Justin Bieber Dream." *New York Times*. 3 Jan. 2010: 1. *Newspaper Source Plus*. Ebsco. Web. 30 Aug. 2011.

9. *Justin Bieber: Never Say Never*. Dir. Jon M. Chu. Perf. Justin Bieber, Pattie Mallette, Scooter Braun. Paramount Home Entertainment, 2011. DVD.

CHAPTER 6. BIEBERMANIA

1. Claire Suddath. "Pop Star 2.0." *Time*. 17 May 2010: 49–50. *MAS Ultra-School Edition*. Ebsco. Web. 30 Aug. 2011.

2. Joey Bartolomeo. "Boy Wonder." *People*. 19 Apr. 2010: 66–72. *Academic Search Premier*. Ebsco. Web. 30 Aug. 2011.

3. Vanessa Grigoriadis. "The Adventure of Super Boy." *Rolling Stone*. 3 March 2011: 52–58. *MAS Ultra-School Edition*. Ebsco. Web. 14 Aug. 2011.

4. Marc Shapiro. *Justin Bieber: The Fever!* New York: St. Martin's Griffin, 2010. Print. 12.

5. Jonathon Gatehouse. "What's Really Going on Under All That Hair." *Maclean's*. 26 July 2010: 44–47. *MAS Ultra-School Edition*. Ebsco. Web. 30 Aug. 2011.

6. James Parker. "Daydream Believer." *The Atlantic* March. 2011: 38–39. *MasterFILE Premier*. Ebsco. Web. 30 Aug. 2011.

CHAPTER 7. SWEET SIXTEEN

1. Jocelyn Vena. "Justin Bieber Releases 'U Smile,' Announces Summer Tour Dates." *MTV.* MTV, 16 Mar. 2010. Web. 11 Sept. 2011.

2. Dave Itzkoff. "Chaos Continues to Follow Justin Bieber." *New York Times*. 29 Apr. 2010: 2. *Newspaper Source Plus*. Ebsco. Web. 30 Aug. 2011.

3. Walker Simon. "Justin Bieber Among Black Entertainment Nominees." *Reuters* 18 May 2010. Web. 11 Sept. 2011.

CHAPTER 8. HEADLINER

1. "Quotes of the Day." *Time World*. Time, 22 Nov. 2010. Web. 30 Aug. 2011.

2. Jon Caramanica. "Cover to Cover: The Why and Wherefore." *New York Times*. New York Times Company, 19 Nov. 2010. Web. 18 Oct. 2011.

CHAPTER 9. KEEPING IT GOING

1. Dave Itzkoff. "'My World' and Welcome to It." *New York Times*. 8 Feb. 2011: 1. *Newspaper Source Plus*. Ebsco. Web. 30 Aug. 2011.

2. Vanessa Grigoriadis. "The Adventure of Super Boy." *Rolling Stone*. 3 March 2011: 52–58. *MAS Ultra-School Edition*. Ebsco. Web. 14 Aug. 2011.

3. Shirley Halperin. "Justin Bieber: 'With Time Off, I'm Able to Think, Pray and Grow Up.'" *Hollywood Reporter*. Hollywood Reporter, 20 July 2011. Web. 14 Aug. 2011.

4. Ibid

5. Ibid.

6. Jonathon Gatehouse. "A Very Sweet Sixteen." *Maclean's*. 13 Dec. 2010: 86. *MasterFILE Premier*. Ebsco. Web. 13 Aug. 2011.

INDEX

ABOUT THE AUTHOR

Valerie Bodden is a freelance author and editor. She has written more than 100 children's nonfiction books. Her books have received positive reviews from *School Library Journal*, *Booklist*, *Children's Literature*, *ForeWord Magazine*, *Horn Book Guide*, *VOYA*, and *Library Media Connection*. Valerie lives in Wisconsin with her husband and their four children.

PHOTO CREDITS